IDEAS IN F

Oedipus Complex

Robert M. Young

Series editor: Ivan Ward

ICON BOOKS UK

TOTEM BOOKS USA

Published in the UK in 2001
by Icon Books Ltd., Grange Road,
Duxford, Cambridge CB2 4QF
E-mail: info@iconbooks.co.uk
www.iconbooks.co.uk

Published in the USA in 2001
by Totem Books
Inquiries to: Icon Books Ltd.,
Grange Road, Duxford
Cambridge CB2 4QF, UK

Sold in the UK, Europe, South Africa
and Asia by Faber and Faber Ltd.,
3 Queen Square, London WC1N 3AU
or their agents

Distributed to the trade in the USA
by National Book Network Inc.,
4720 Boston Way, Lanham,
Maryland 20706

Distributed in the UK, Europe,
South Africa and Asia by
Macmillan Distribution Ltd.,
Houndmills, Basingstoke RG21 6XS

Distributed in Canada by
Penguin Books Canada,
10 Alcorn Avenue, Suite 300,
Toronto, Ontario M4V 3B2

Published in Australia in 2001
by Allen & Unwin Pty. Ltd.,
PO Box 8500, 83 Alexander Street,
Crows Nest, NSW 2065

ISBN 1 84046 274 4

Text copyright © 2001 Robert M. Young

The author has asserted his moral rights.

Series editor: Ivan Ward

Typesetting by Hands Fotoset

Printed and bound in the UK by
Cox & Wyman Ltd., Reading

It has always seemed odd to me that the Oedipus myth and complex should lie at the heart of our humanity. It strikes me as so eccentric, so weird, in the same way that being sensually excited by dangling bits of fat with nipples on them, or an enlarged vein with a sac beneath it, seems undignified and comical. But there it is: evolution, culture and fashion have left us this way, with sexuality and the Oedipal triangle intermingled and as lifelong unconscious preoccupations which have ramifications throughout both personal and large-scale history.

Freudian Ideas of the Oedipus Complex

The idea of the Oedipus complex was developed by Sigmund Freud around the turn of the twentieth century. He drew on his clinical experience, his self-analysis and the Greek cycle of plays by Sophocles – in particular, *Oedipus Rex*, in which Oedipus kills his father and marries his mother with disastrous consequences. That is, Oedipus breaks the taboo against incest, and tragedy ensues. In practice, the Oedipus complex means that children from about three to six years have intense loving feelings towards one parent and seek to possess that parent exclusively, while having strong negative feelings towards the other parent. Boys love their mothers and hate their fathers. Girls do too, but they move on to hate their mothers and to seek to possess their fathers. At the unconscious level, these feelings are sexual towards the desired parent and murderous towards the same-sex parent. If all goes well in psychological development, the child comes to see how he or she benefits from the parental union and learns to contain possessive and hostile feelings. Out of the resolution of the Oedipus complex comes the conscience, or 'superego'. Children learn not to act on violent impulses and to obey the rules of civilisation and the conventions of culture and society, the incest taboo being the most basic of these. The intense Oedipal feelings get reprised in adolescence, when teenagers are typically rebellious, experiment with their sexual identities and make trouble, sometimes serious trouble, for their parents. Think of the anguished lack of communication between James Dean and his father in the film *Rebel Without a Cause* (1955), or the hopeless breakdown of communication between father and daughter, and the neighbour's son and his father, in the film *American Beauty* (1999).

People who do not successfully work through their

Oedipus complex are left immature, unable to get on, feel hung up about one or both parents, get involved in acting out rather than containing their psychological difficulties and/or experience stasis in their careers and relationships, have impaired impulse control and difficulty with authority and are prey to all sorts of other troubles. Think of the stymied life of Brick Pollitt (played by Paul Newman) in his relationships with his wife (Elizabeth Taylor) and his patriarchal father, 'Big Daddy' (Burl Ives), in the film version of Tennessee Williams' play *Cat on a Hot Tin Roof* (1955), released in 1958. The vicissitudes of an unresolved Oedipus complex often get passed down the generations. Having a bad relationship with one or both parents makes one's own parenting more difficult. Some also say that the vicissitudes of the Oedipus complex affect sexual orientation. A too strong attachment to a domineering mother, coupled with a weak or absent father, was a fundamentally important factor in the aetiology of male homosexuality in *Suddenly Last Summer* (1958), another play by Tennessee Williams. Others hotly dispute this link.

These are weighty matters, ones which Freud claimed in *Civilization and Its Discontents* (1930) provide the historical and emotional foundations of culture, law, civility and decency. Once again, what are the bare elements? First, there is the Oedipal triangle, wherein a child somewhere between three-and-a-half and six wants exclusive access to the parent of the opposite sex – physically, emotionally and intellectually – and has to come to terms with the prior claims of the same-sex parent. The child fears retaliation and soon begins to feel guilty for his incestuous desire and murderous impulses. Guilt reveals the presence of the superego, which Freud described as the heir to the Oedipus complex. The whole thing comes up again in adolescence, with respect to sexuality and to authority, and may arise again when one or the other parent dies. Patients who have not negotiated these rites of passage have unresolved Oedipal problems. One of the big ones that inhibits achievement and satisfaction is fear of surpassing a parent, leading to fear of retaliation for so-called 'Oedipal triumph'. Another is the risk of believing that one can be an adult without growing up emotionally, expecting fairy-tale or magical solutions to life's problems.[1]

In addition to my reservations about the Oedipus complex in general, I have also been slow to accept

the centrality of the Oedipal triangle in psycho-
analysis and psychotherapy – to realise that the
analytic space is an Oedipal space. Patients experience their therapists as parental figures and fall in love
with them as they once did with their parents. Within
the analytic frame, the familial Oedipal dynamic is
reprised.[2] The analytic relationship involves continually offering incest and continually declining it
in the name of analytic abstinence and the hope of a
relationship that transcends incestuous desires.
Breaking the analytic frame invariably involves the
risk of child abuse, and sleeping with patients or ex-
patients is precisely that.

Martin Bergmann puts some of these points very
nicely in an essay on transference love, wherein the
patient falls romantically in love with the therapist.
He says:

*In the analytic situation, the early images are made
consciuus and thereby deprived of their energizing
potential. In analysis, the uncovering of the incestuous
fixation behind transference love loosens the incestuous ties and prepares the way for a future love free
from the need to repeat oedipal triangulation. Under
conditions of health the infantile prototypes merely*

energize the new falling in love while in neurosis they also evoke the incest taboo and needs for new triangulation that repeat the triangle of the oedipal state.[3]

With respect to patients who get involved with ex-therapists, he says that they claim that 'unlike the rest of humanity I am entitled to disobey the incest taboo, circumventing the work of mourning, and possess my parent sexually. I am entitled to do so because I suffered so much or simply because I am an exception'.[4] From the therapist's point of view, 'When the transference relationship becomes a sexual one, it represents symbolically and unconsciously the fulfilment of the wish that the infantile love object will not be given up and that incestuous love can be refound in reality'.[5] This is a variant on the Pygmalion theme. The analytic relationship works only to the extent that the therapist shows, in Freud's words, 'that he is proof against every temptation'.[6]

Looking further into the Oedipal dynamic as experiences in the clinical psychoanalytic relationship, one finds the phantasy of the copulating parental couple with which the patient has to come to terms – hopefully moving from an unconscious phantasy of something violent and feared to a more benign one, in the lee of which he or she can feel safe, benefiting from the parents' union. It was my clinical practice that slowly eroded my conceptual scepticism about the Oedipus complex. It simply came up before me in clinical material again and again. Some of my patients are stuck because they have *no* phantasy of their parents together and believe that they are in bed between the parents, preventing them from getting together, and cannot get on with relationships themselves because of the harm they unconsciously believe they have caused. Stasis, longing and lack of fulfilment are the likely results.

A Closer Look at Oedipal Dynamics

Let's turn to a more detailed exploration of psycho-analytic formulations of the Oedipal dynamic and start with a definite developmental scheme, the one which constitutes the classical chronological story of orthodox Freudianism, as modified and enriched by Karl Abraham and, some would say, Erik Erikson. We begin with primary narcissism and pass through several successive phases of focus on particular bodily zones: oral, anal, phallic and genital – oral for the first year and a half, anal for the next year and a half, and phallic beginning towards the close of the third year.[7]

As I have said, the classical Oedipal period is from age three-and-a-half to six (some say five). This leads on to the formation of the superego and a period of relative latency, during which boys are quintessentially boyish and horrid, with their bikes, hobbies and play, and girls are sugar and spice and all things nice, playing nurse and mummy, or so it is said.[8] Things get fraught again in adolescence when biological changes coincide with agonising problems about gender identity,[9] sexual exploration and maturation, conflict with parents, competitiveness and achievement. Erik Erikson spells out a further set of stages, beginning with a psychosocial moratorium in late adolescence, followed by young adulthood, full adulthood and mature age, the last of which he characterises as a period in which the central conflict is between integrity, on the one hand, and disgust and despair, on the other.[10]

A detailed chronology of the phases of the Oedipus complex is spelled out in Humberto Nagera's orthodox Freudian exposition of *Basic Psychoanalytic Concepts on the Libido Theory* (1969).[11] I find it remarkable that there is not here or in Freud's writings or in Laplanche and Pontalis' *The Language of Psychoanalysis* (1973),[12] an agreed, straightforward account.[13] This is particularly true of the female Oedipus complex:

Throughout history people have knocked their heads against the riddle of the nature of femininity . . . Nor will you have escaped worrying over this problem – those of you who are men; to those of you who are women this will not apply – you are yourselves the problem.[14]

Freud's impish humour does not obscure the fact that he is looking at femininity from a masculine point of view, and this has been the basis of much criticism of his idea within psychoanalysis and beyond. With regard to the female Oedipus complex, he was faced with a problem. Since all children – both boys and girls – are originally attached to the mother, how is it that the female child turns to her father to become a 'daddy's girl'? Something must break the bond with the mother. Freud's answer brought opprobrium on his head from feminists and traditionalists alike. The girl is said to discover that she has no penis, to suffer from 'penis envy' and to look to her mother to supply her with one. When this is not forthcoming, she is disappointed. She blames her mother for the sense of deficiency, turns to the father in search of one, and remains ungratified until she gets a symbolic penis in the form of a baby.[15] For the boy, it is the 'castration complex' that turns him away from his mother; fear of the consequences of his incestuous desires. For a girl child, the female version of the castration complex – penis envy – is what catapults her into the Oedipus complex. But since she is already 'castrated' and has suffered the fate that the little boy is trying to prevent, the rivalry with the mother takes on a different, and perhaps more lasting, quality. Freud argued that the fact that the girl's Oedipus complex is resolved much more slowly, more gently and less brutally and abruptly than the boy's, accounts for the fact that girls' consciences are less brittle than those of males. It has also been suggested that some men – black slaves and post-colonials – are perpetually under such real or symbolic threat of emasculation that they never resolve their castration complexes and that this (along with poor economic prospects) may help explain the tendency on the part of some to be inconstant and to avoid familial responsibilities.[16]

The orthodox story of the Oedipus complex in its various forms is much-disputed, most obviously and appropriately by feminists (some of whom, for example, counter the idea of female penis envy with the notion of males having 'womb envy') and also by gays and lesbians and Lacanians and I don't know who-all. It is called too naturalistic and biologistic, too literally linked to parts of the body, too deterministic. In the real world of human development, as Freud well knew, there is an infinite number of outcomes to this momentous story, for both men and women – an infinite number of partial resolutions, compromises and sublimations. It should also be said that Freud was forever revising his views on both the male and female Oedipus complex and that his account of the female one is the messier and less adequately theorised of the two. As I shall show below, there is a more abstract and Kleinian version of Oedipal dynamics which suffers less from being found implausible.

The debates about the details of the direct and indirect Oedipus complex and the role of bisexuality in the Oedipal process are many and labyrinthine and can be followed in the abundant literature. I shall not detail them here, since I believe that an overview should paint on a broader canvas and because there are two sorts of issues about the Oedipus complex which are at the centre of recent debates, and summaries of them are not readily accessible: Kleinian ideas about the Oedipus complex, and anti-naturalistic positions about sexuality which challenge the whole idea of a biologically given, psychosexual developmental scheme.[17]

Before turning to those topics, however, I want to linger over the classical Freudian story. Freud called the Oedipus complex 'the core complex' or 'the nuclear complex' of every neurosis. In a footnote added to the 1920 edition of *Three Essays on Sexuality*, he made it clear that the Oedipus complex is the immovable foundation stone on which the whole edifice of psychoanalysis is based:

It has justly been said that the Oedipus complex is the nuclear complex of the neuroses, and constitutes the essential part of their content. It represents the peak of infantile sexuality, which, through its after-effects, exercises a decisive influence on the sexuality of adults. Every new arrival on this planet is faced with the task of mastering the Oedipus complex; anyone who fails to do so falls a victim to neurosis. With the progress of psycho-analytic studies the importance of the Oedipus complex has become more and more clearly evident; its recognition has become the

*shibboleth that distinguishes the adherents of psycho-
analysis from its opponents.*[18]

In the first published reference to the incest taboo in
1905 (he had written about the 'horror of incest' and
incest as 'anti-social' in an unpublished draft in 1897),
Freud refers to it as 'a cultural demand made by
society' that may get passed on by organic inheritance, and adds in a footnote of 1915, 'Psychoanalytic investigation shows, however, how intensely
the individual struggles with the temptation to incest
during his period of growth and how frequently the
barrier is transgressed in phantasy and even in
reality.'[19] In both the development of the individual
and the history of mankind, Freud identified the
incest taboo as the basis of all other prohibitions.
Guilt was the essential weapon in the struggle against
uncivilised, rapacious impulses, and sublimation of
sexual energies provided the energy for *all* of culture
and civilisation, concepts that he disdained to
distinguish: 'Incest is anti-social and civilisation
consists of the progressive renunciation of it.'[20] The
rapacious, sexually polymorphous 'primal father',
the patriarch of the 'primal horde', was opposed and
killed by his sons, and thus was established the taboo

against incest, the foundation stone of all moral and cultural prohibitions. 'We cannot get away from the assumption that man's sense of guilt springs from the Oedipus complex and was acquired at the killing of the father by the brothers banned together.'[21] The price we pay for the advance of civilisation 'is a loss of happiness through the heightening of the sense of guilt'. He calls this 'the final conclusion of our investigation', thus making vivid the juxtaposition of civilisation and discontent in the title of the book: civilisation *causes* discontents.[22] He saw all of the vast panorama of human history as being acted out in the emotional space between Eros and Thanatos – the constructive impulse to love and create, and the aggressive impulse to destroy and die.

Freud claimed that the Oedipus complex is universal, and there have been heated debates, some involving anthropological fieldwork, about this. These debates have become pretty arcane, and I have the impression that orthodox Freudians have stretched things a long way in the hope of retaining some version of universality of the Oedipus complex, while critics have been scathing about them and about Freud's historical speculations about the 'primal horde'.[23] We are privileged to have a useful summary of these debates in *Oedipus Ubiquitous: The Family Complex in World Folk Literature* (1996), by Allen W. Johnson and Douglass Price-Williams. They review the issues and conclude that the complex as specified by Freud is prevalent in advanced, authoritarian societies, while a much looser version involving inter-generational conflict is widespread among the 139 folk tales they review, though more of the ones similar to Freud's account are about boys than girls.[24] Freud's very concrete claims about this or that body part fare less well than the general inter-generational conflict. There is also interesting psychoanalytic work by Alan Roland (1988) which shows important cultural differences in this matter in India (where conflict in sons and fathers is deeply taboo) and Japan (where deference is deeply embedded in women's personalities).

I want to make two more points about Freud's views which I offer as counterweights to the mistaken belief that Freud was too reductionist and biologistic and left little space for historical relativity. First, although he saw the Oedipus complex as universal and rooted in our biological inheritance, he also saw its resolution as freeing us to some extent from that very heritage. Freud wrote:

Otto Rank, in a large volume on the incest complex (1912), has produced evidence of the surprising fact that the choice of subject matter, especially for dramatic works, is principally determined by the ambit of what psychoanalysis has termed the 'Oedipus Complex'. By working it over with the greatest variety of modifications, distortions and disguises, the dramatist seeks to deal with his own most personal relations to this emotional theme. It is in attempting to master the Oedipus Complex – that is to say a person's emotional attitude towards his family, or in the narrower sense towards his father and mother – that individual neurotics come to grief, and for this reason that complex habitually forms the nucleus of their neurosis. [25]

This developmental task which faces each individual is connected for Freud with universal features of human nature. He continues:

It does not owe its importance to any unintelligible conjunction; the emphasis laid upon the relation of children to their parents is an expression of the biological facts that the young of the human race pass through a long period of dependence and are slow in reaching maturity, as well as that their capacity for love undergoes a complicated course of development. Consequently, the overcoming of the Oedipus complex coincides with the most efficient way of mastering the archaic, animal heritage of humanity. It is true that that heritage comprises all the forces that are required for the subsequent cultural development of the individual, but they must first be sorted out and worked over. This archaic heirloom is not fit to be used for the purposes of social life in the form in which it is inherited by the individual.[26]

Second, the universality of the Oedipus complex does not mean immunity from historical development and cultural relativity in how Oedipal forces are expressed. Freud compares social mores at the time of Sophocles with those at the time of Shakespeare. Immediately after the first mention of the Oedipus complex in *The Interpretation of Dreams* (1900), in which he advocates its universal nature, Freud emphasises the historical specificity of this momentous theme:

There is an unmistakable indication in the text of Sophocles' tragedy itself that the legend of Oedipus sprang from some primaeval dream-material which had as its content the distressing disturbance of a child's relation to his parents owing to the first stirrings of sexuality . . .

Another of the great creations of tragic poetry, Shakespeare's Hamlet, *has its roots in the same soil as* Oedipus Rex. *But the changed treatment of the same material reveals the whole difference in the mental life of these two widely separated epochs of civilisation: the secular advance of repression in the emotional life of mankind. In the* Oedipus *the child's wishful phantasy that underlies it is brought into the open and realised as it would be in a dream. In* Hamlet *it remains repressed; and – just as in the case of neurosis – we only learn of its existence from its inhibiting consequences . . . Hamlet is able to do anything – except take vengeance on the man who did away with his father and took that father's place with his mother, the man who shows him the repressed wishes of his own childhood realised. Thus the loathing which should drive him on to revenge is replaced in him by self-reproaches, by scruples of conscience, which remind him that he himself is literally no better than the sinner whom he is to punish.*[27]

Kleinian Ideas

How do specifically Kleinian ideas relate to all this? First, Melanie Klein famously claimed to find what she called 'the Oedipal situation' much earlier in life, along with persecuting ideas from the superego, long before a Freudian would grant that there could *be* a superego. She found the internalised idea of the copulating parental couple – for ill or good – in very early phantasies.

Klein is Freud's most assiduous follower with respect to the dual instinct theory (Eros–Thanatos) and the sombre lessons of Freud's theory of civilisation and its discontents. But there is a quite fundamental divergence between them with respect to development, structures and, indeed, all of the signposts in the inner world that help Freudians to find their way about. Kleinian ideas in this area help us to see why it is so hard to get hold of Klein at all. I am going to spell out the history and present situation with respect to the Kleinian tradition on the Oedipus complex, but I shall offer my overall conclusion now.

I think it's a matter of background and foreground. This may appear at first glance a small matter, but I think it is of fundamental significance. At first I thought that developmental chronology and stages didn't matter at all for Klein. I thought the structural hypothesis of id, ego and superego[28] didn't matter to her either, but I was mistaken. These concepts are there – all of them. So are those of the oral, anal, phallic and genital stages, as well as the Oedipus complex, but they are not in the foreground. They are background. What is in the foreground is the interplay of emotions and positions. A 'position' for Klein is a constellation of anxieties and defences, object relations and impulses.[29] The fundamental dichotomy is between Eros and Thanatos, which, in turn, give us paired emotions such as love and hate, gratitude and envy – all directed to whole-object and part-object relations.

There is another general point to be put alongside this one about positions and emotions. It is that the primitive is never transcended in the way it is in the Freudian developmental scheme. In particular, psychotic anxieties continue to break through integrated perceptions, leading to a perpetual oscillation between two fundamental ways of being in the unconscious – the paranoid-schizoid and depressive positions, the latter of which is characterised by integrated, more mature thinking in relation to whole objects, whereas part-object relations dominate the paranoid-schizoid position. The two positions were eventually linked with a double-headed arrow to show the oscillation between them: $Ps \leftrightarrow D$. It is because the primitive continues to dominate that the developmental scheme is background, while the interplay of emotions is foreground. This notion about foreground and background is supported in the argument of a paper by Ruth Stein (1990) to which I will return below. I am suggesting that the problem of finding one's way in the Kleinian inner world is to a considerable extent explained by the fact that they have taken the signposts down, rather as the British did when they expected Hitler to invade. The result is that feelings are rushing around without the benefit of the sorts of roadmaps, boundaries and tramlines that make Freudians feel safe.

Oedipus Rex

I now want to ponder Oedipus a bit. In the light of all the recent revelations and controversies about child abuse, I had a sudden insight about old *King Oedipus*, the play Aristotle called the perfect tragedy, the inspiration for the other candidate, *Hamlet*.[30] If we ask when Oedipus committed incest, the answers can be seen in a very different light than the usual story gives. What really happened is that having heard from the oracle that his child would murder its father and marry its mother, Laius assaulted his son at birth. In Sophocles' writings, Jocasta tells it like this:

As for the child,
It was not yet three days old, when it was cast out
(By other hands, not his) with riveted ankles
To perish on the empty mountain-side.[31]

'Oedipus', the name he was given by his adoptive parents, Polybus and Meropé, means 'swollen-footed'. When he was older and heard from a drunkard that he was not the son of Polybus, who he believed to be his father, he asked his supposed parents who were distressed that anyone had said this. He went to an oracle:

. . . I went to Pytho;
But came back disappointed of any answer
To the question I asked, having heard instead a tale
Of horror and misery: how I must marry my mother,
And become the parent of a misbegotten brood,
An offence to all mankind – and kill my father.[32]

Oedipus fled from Corinth, 'never to see home again /
That no such horror should ever come to pass',[33] in
order to avoid harming Polybus, his supposed father,
and to avoid sleeping with Meropé, the woman he
believed to be his mother. As he did so, he had a
chance encounter with Laius at a crossroad. Did his
father greet him with open arms? No, he did not. He
tried to bully him over the trivial matter of who
should pass first at a crossroad.

When I came to the place where three roads join, I met
A herald followed by a horse-drawn carriage, and a man
Seated therein, just as you have described.
The leader roughly ordered me out of the way;
And his venerable master joined in with a surly
  command.
It was the driver that thrust me aside, and him I struck,
For I was angry. The old man saw it, leaning from the
  carriage,
Waited until I passed, then, seizing for weapon
The driver's two-pronged goad, struck me on the head.
He paid with interest for his temerity;
Quick as lightning, the staff in this right hand
Did its work; he tumbled headlong out of the carriage,
And every man of them there I killed.[34]

What has Oedipus done except get assaulted at birth and again when he was trying to run away from the Oedipal triangle?[35] Of course, he certainly over-reacted to the bullying, but he was assaulted twice. Then he answers the riddle – about the life cycle ('What walks on four feet then two then three?'), ends the tyranny of the Sphinx, gets the prize (which turns out to be incestuous union with his mother), learns the truth in veiled form from wise, blind old Teiresias, doubts him, pursues the truth relentlessly, and gets it confirmed by servants who were directly involved in the crucial events. Oedipus feels dreadful; Jocasta hangs herself. Oedipus puts out his own eyes and eventually attains wisdom from looking into the inner world. As I read the play, I realise he has had bad, uncontained and uncontaining parents, a far from good enough mother, a grossly and repeatedly abusing father and a bad press, one which could rival our own renditions of couples and triangles. This man was well and truly maltreated and has the scars to prove it.

But as close inspection reveals with respect to many of the abused, this is not the whole story. A very different one can be told about his unconscious. Indeed, there is some evidence that Sophocles was a proto-Kleinian, since, if we look at the inner world, Oedipus will have been having the impulses – which explained, though they did not justify, Laius's behaviour – at a *very* early age. He wasn't committing incest in his mind at three and a half, as he would have if he were a Freudian baby, but straightaway, like a good Kleinian baby. No primary narcissism, as a Freudian would have it, but object relations at birth.

As John Steiner has argued, there is evidence that all the people involved in the tragedy really did know the other story or could easily have worked it out, but they 'turned a blind eye'.[36] I've had another look at the *Theban Plays*, and I am here to tell you that Sophocles must certainly have intuited Klein's 1928 paper, though we cannot be sure about the 1945 one or the 1946 one, where the role of projective identification in the paranoid-schizoid position was fully formulated, thus providing all the elements of the modern Kleinian analogue of the Oedipal story.[37]

Freud and *Oedipus Rex*

It would be a truism to say that this play made a deep impression on Freud, but I think it might benefit us to dwell a moment on that fact. We know that he said to his close interlocutor, Wilhelm Fliess, in 1897, 'I have found in my own case too, falling in love with the mother and jealousy of the father, and I now regard it as a universal event of childhood . . . If that is so, we can understand the riveting power of *Oedipus Rex*'.[38] He tells about seeking out his own family story in that letter and suggests that the same tragic triangle is at the heart of the inter-generational dynamics in *Hamlet*.[39]

Freud wrote of *Oedipus* in *The Interpretation of Dreams*.

If Oedipus Rex *moves a modern audience no less than it did the contemporary Greek one, the explanation can only be that its effect does not lie in the contrast between destiny and human will, but is to be looked for in the particular nature of the material on which that contrast is exemplified. There must be something which makes a voice within us ready to recognize the compelling force of destiny in the* Oedipus, *while we can dismiss as merely arbitrary such dispositions as are laid down in . . . other modern tragedies of destiny. And a factor of this kind is in fact involved in the story of King Oedipus. His destiny moves us only because it might have been ours – because the oracle laid the same curse upon us before our birth as upon him. It is the fate of all of us, perhaps, to direct our first sexual impulse toward our mother and our first hatred and our first murderous wish against our father. Our dreams convince us that this is so. King Oedipus, who slew his father Laius and married his mother Jocasta, merely shows us the fulfilment of our own childhood wishes. But, more fortunate than he, we have meanwhile succeeded, in so far as we have not become psychoneurotics, in detaching our sexual impulses from our mothers and forgetting our jealousy of our fathers. Here is one in whom these primaeval wishes of our childhood have been fulfilled. And we shrink back from him with the whole force of the repression by which those wishes have since that time been held down within us. While the poet, as he unravels the past, brings to light the guilt of Oedipus, he is at the same time compelling us to recognise our own inner minds, in which those same impulses, though suppressed, are still to be found. The contrast with which the closing Chorus leaves us confronted –*

> *. . . fix on Oedipus your eyes,*
> *Who resolved the dark enigma, noblest*
> *   champion and most wise.*
> *Like a star his envied fortune mounted beaming*

far and wide:
Now he sinks in seas of anguish, whelmed
    beneath a raging tide . . .

– strikes a warning at ourselves and our pride, at us who since our childhood have grown so wise and so mighty in our own eyes. Like Oedipus, we live in ignorance of these wishes, repugnant to morality, which have been forced upon us by Nature, and after their revelation we may all of us well seek to close our eyes to the scenes of our childhood.[40]

He added this note in 1919: 'Later studies have shown that the "Oedipus complex" which was touched upon in the above paragraphs in the *Interpretation of Dreams*, throws a light of undreamt-of importance on the history of the human race and the evolution of religion and morality'.[41] Freud had added the term 'complex' under the influence of Carl Jung in 1910, and, as we have seen, in *Totem and Taboo* claimed that an actual killing of a father by a primal horde lay at the foundation of human history.[42]

Freud's own family constellation was multi-generationally confused. His father was twenty years older than his mother and already a grandfather via a grown son from his first marriage when Freud was born. That son and another were at least as old as the new bride. Freud was the eldest son of his family but the youngest child in the broader family group. The other two young children were, respectively, a year older and the same age, but his nephew and niece. A brother once said to him that he was of the third generation, not the second, with respect to his father.[43] (I am reminded of a novelty song on the Hit Parade when I was a boy, which told of family relations and re-marriages so complicated that the singer could logically claim, 'I'm my own grandpa!') It is no wonder that when Freud was reflecting on finishing secondary school, the one bit of study he singled out for mention was *Oedipus Rex*, in which he came first in his class on the basis of a translation from the Greek of the opening speech of the priest, beseeching Oedipus to deliver the Thebans from a complex and bewildering pestilence which was caused by the breaking of the inter-generational incest taboo.[44]

The significance of all this was driven home dramatically when Freud's disciples presented him with a medallion on his fiftieth birthday. On one side was Freud's portrait in profile, and on the other side a design of Oedipus answering the Sphinx, with this line from the closing passage of the play: 'Who knew the famous riddles and was a man most mighty.' When Freud read it he became pale and agitated about an uncanny coincidence between this tribute and his own fantasies. As a student he had strolled around the arcade of the University of Vienna, inspecting the busts of the famous professors. He had imagined his own bust there in the future with that exact inscription. His identification with Oedipus could not have been more complete.[45] Even Freud was shaken by feelings of Oedipal triumph. In the light of this life-long preoccupation, it is all the more striking that he never wrote a systematic exposition of his mature views on the Oedipus complex – a concept which was, by his own account, the centrepiece of his theory.

Exposition of Klein's Views

I want to turn now to an exposition of Kleinian views on the Oedipus complex. Klein's answer to the question, 'When did Oedipus commit incest?', is that he did it from the beginning, at least in unconscious phantasy. I will offer you both a clear and a diffuse version of this point. The sharp one can be found in all the various attempts to delineate Kleinian accounts from Freudian ones. They all depend on the developmental scheme I outlined above and to holding fast to the chronology that that implies. If it were not for this distinct schema, there would be little or no conflict between the conceptions. If you read through the 'Controversial Discussions' between the Kleinians and the rest of the members of the British Psychoanalytic Society in the early 1940s, the point comes up again and again that Klein is thought to be, as they repeatedly put it, 'depreciating' the classical Oedipus complex which occurs at three or beyond.[46] Klein denies this but acknowledges that there is a conflict. It is a conflict about what can be in the child's mind very early in life. As I have already said more than once, it is also a conflict about structure and chronology, foreground and background, how the mind works and how to think about it, but I'll return to that later.

Let's start with a simple rendition of Klein on the Oedipus complex.[47] Klein makes a distinction between what she calls 'the Oedipal situation', which recurs throughout life, and the classical Oedipus complex of Freud: 'According to Freud, genital desires emerge and a definite object choice takes place during the phallic phase, which extends from about three to five years of age, and is contemporaneous with the Oedipus complex.'[48] The superego and the sense of guilt are sequelae of the Oedipus complex.[49] Klein's view is that emotional and sexual development '*from early infancy onwards* includes genital sensations and trends, which constitute the first stages of the inverted [desire towards same-sex parent; aggression towards opposite sex one] and positive Oedipus complex; they are experienced under the primacy of oral libido and mingle with urethral and anal desires and phantasies. The libidinal stages overlap from the first months of life onwards.'[50] She dates the superego from the oral phase. 'Under the sway of phantasy life and of conflicting emotions, the child at every stage of libidinal organization introjects his objects – primarily his parents – and builds up the super-ego from these elements . . . All the factors which have a bearing on his object relations play a part from the beginning in the build-up of the super-ego'.[51]

At first, it is not the parent as a whole that is introjected but only particular aspects, i.e., significant part-objects:

The first introjected object, the mother's breast, forms

the basis of the super-ego . . . The earliest feelings of guilt in both sexes derive from the oral-sadistic desires to devour the mother, and primarily her breasts (Abraham). It is therefore in infancy that feelings of guilt arise. Guilt does not emerge when the Oedipus complex comes to an end, but is rather one of the factors which from the beginning mould its course and affect its outcome.[52]

Klein's final remarks begin with a passage which supports my impression that she intermingles concepts which would be carefully distinguished in a Freudian developmental scheme:

The sexual development of the child is inextricably bound up with his object relations and with all the emotions which from the beginning mould his attitude to mother and father. Anxiety, guilt and depressive feelings are intrinsic elements of the child's emotional life and therefore permeate the child's early object relations, which consist of the relation to actual people as well as to their representatives in the inner world. From these introjected figures – the child's identifications – the super-ego develops and in turn influences the relation to both parents and the whole sexual development. Thus emotional and sexual development, object relations and super-ego development interact from the beginning.[53]

She concludes: 'The infant's emotional life, the early defences built up under the stress between love, hatred and guilt, and the vicissitudes of the child's identifications – all these are topics which may well occupy analytic research for a long time to come.'[54] As with Freud, it is striking that although she lived for a further fifteen years and remained intellectually productive, Klein did not provide an integration of her views on this topic with her mature versions of other characteristically Kleinian preoccupations.

Recent Kleinian Ideas

'The Oedipus Complex in the Light of Early Anxieties' (1945) was published a year before Klein coined a term to characterise what was almost certainly her most profound idea, the mechanism which she called 'a particular form of identification which establishes the prototype of an aggressive object relation. I suggest for these processes the term "projective identification"'.[55] This lies at the heart of the paranoid-schizoid position, in which splitting, projective mechanisms and part-object relations predominate. One can see these mechanisms at work in racism and other forms of virulent hatred in which a despised out-group becomes the repository of disowned and projected 'bad' characteristics. Once again, this configuration is in a dynamic relation with the depressive position, in which whole-object relations, concern for the object and integration predominate. What has happened in the subsequent research to which Klein alluded is that these ways of thinking have been brought into relationship with one another. As David Bell puts it:

The primitive Oedipal conflict described by Klein takes place in the paranoid-schizoid position when the infant's world is widely split and relations are mainly to part objects. This means that any object which threatens the exclusive possession of the idealised breast/mother is felt as a persecutor and has projected into it all the hostile feelings deriving from pregenital impulses.[56]

If development proceeds satisfactorily, secure relations with good internal objects lead to integration, healing of splits and taking back projections:

The mother is then, so to speak, free to be involved with a third object in a loving intercourse which, instead of being a threat, becomes the foundation of a secure relation to internal and external reality. The capacity to represent internally the loving intercourse between the parents as whole objects results, through the ensuing identifications, in the capacity for full genital maturity. For Klein, the resolution of the Oedipus complex and the achievement of the depressive position refer to the same phenomena viewed from different perspectives.[57]

Ronald Britton puts it very elegantly:

[T]he two situations are inextricably intertwined in such a way that one cannot be resolved without the other: we resolve the Oedipus complex by working through the depressive position and the depressive position by working through the Oedipus complex.[58]

We are provided here with a key to translating between the Freudian and Kleinian conceptual schemes. In both frames of reference, the child comes to terms with his or her place within the family triangle (whether this involves two real parents or one, with the idea of a third person held in the mind of the caring parent). In the recent work of Kleinians, this way of thinking has been considerably broadened. For example, it has been applied to development of the ability to symbolise and learn from experience. Integration of the depressive position – which we can now see as resolution of the Oedipus complex – is the *sine qua non* of the development of 'a capacity for symbol formation and rational thought'.[59] Greater knowledge of the object 'includes awareness of its continuity of existence in time and space and also therefore of the other relationships of the object implied by that realization. The Oedipal situation exemplifies that knowledge. Hence the depressive position cannot be worked through without working through the Oedipus complex and vice versa.'[60] Britton also sees 'the depressive position and the Oedipal situation as never finished but as having to be re-worked in each new life situation, at each stage of development, and with each major addition to experience or knowledge.'[61]

This way of looking at the Oedipal situation also offers a way of thinking of self-knowledge or insight:

The primal family triangle provides the child with two links connecting him separately with each parent and confronts him with the link between them which excludes him. Initially this parental link is conceived in primitive part-object terms and in the modes of his own oral, anal and genital desires, and in terms of his hatred expressed in oral, anal and genital terms. If the link between the parents perceived in love and hate can be tolerated in the child's mind, it provides him with a prototype for an object relationship of a third kind in which he is a witness and not a participant. A third position then comes into existence from which object relationships can be observed. Given this, we can also envisage being observed. This provides us with a capacity for seeing ourselves in interaction with others and for entertaining another point of view whilst retaining our own, for reflecting on ourselves whilst being ourselves.[62]

I find this very helpful – indeed, profound.

I had an odd experience while I was working out what I had to say about this matter. I knew that an important source would be the 'Controversial Discussions' in the 1940s when Kleinians and Freudians debated, as I confidently supposed, this very matter.[63] I had done research in the compendious volume on these debates with respect to other topics:

in particular, phantasy and psychotic anxieties, which have huge index entries – a whole page in one case and a half-page in the other. 'Oedipus complex' has only a few lines. After reading all the relevant passages, it took me the longest time to figure out this apparent inconsistency. The answer is that they are not separate topics. That is, the Kleinians were challenging the neat developmental scheme of classical and neo-Freudians. They were drawing attention to the *content* of early emotional processes, whereas Freudians tended to focus on scientistic models and metapsychological presentations of their *forms.* What I think was really novel and breathtaking about what Klein and her colleagues were reflecting upon was the primitive ferocity of the content of unconscious phantasies and psychotic anxieties which, as Hinshelwood puts it, lie 'beneath the classical Oedipus complex'.[64]

This role for unconscious threats is particularly true of the combined parent figure and the terrified phantasies – normal but psychotic anxieties – associated with it,[65] as well as the child's feelings about his or her role and situation – at risk, excluded, responsible. I experience a number of my patients as in stasis because of inactivity in this space due to depression, preoccupation or estrangement between the parents. (André Green has written a moving paper on this.[66]) They cannot get on with life, because there is no living relationship, no benign combined parent figure in the lee of which they can feel contained and can prosper. Sometimes they stay very still, lest the stasis give way to something far worse.

I often feel that the controversialists in the Freud–Klein debates were talking past one another – the Freudians about actual parents and conscious feelings and the Kleinians about internal objects, part-objects and utterly primitive unconscious phantasies of a particularly distressing and preverbal kind. The analogy occurs to me between the truths Oedipus thought he was seeking and the deeper ones which eventually emerged and which Steiner suggests were unconsciously known all along. One of the main features of recent Kleinian developments in this area is that the Oedipal situation is increasingly being seen as concerned with the prerequisites of knowledge, containment and that which is being contained. The focus changes to the riddle of the Sphinx and the search for the truth of origins which represent the Oedipal quest in its widest sense – that of the need to know at a deeper level: *epistemophilia*.

I now want to turn to those matters to which I promised to revert. There are a number of points to be made. First, Klein's views on the Oedipal situation and the Oedipus complex were developing in ways which interacted with the development of other major concepts, in particular, the depressive position, the paranoid-schizoid position and projective identification. Something parallel happened with Freud's conscious, preconscious and unconscious (deep categories of topography) and id, ego and superego (important but not so deep categories of structure). Freud never explicitly replaced his topographic metapsychology with the structural one, nor did he make a clear distinction between the superego and the ego ideal.[67] Evolving theories are not tidy.

Second, my signposts about background and foreground can now be applied to the relationship between primitive processes, positions and emotions, on the one hand, and developmental schemes, chronology, topography and the structural hypothesis, on the other. Klein had no quarrel with the background, but it was not her central concern. It was the depths of the id and the unconscious that preoccupied her. People would take her to be writing and speaking in unorthodox ways about structures, when she was burrowing away at the core of a child's being. What was foreground for Klein – the interplay of unconscious feelings – was background for the Freudians, or they were silent about it, preferring to present things in scientistic analogies of forces, energies, structures, adaptations, etc.[68] Klein often chucks in the whole caboodle: the phrase 'oral, anal and phallic' recurs throughout her writings, as does 'mingle', as if she were making a salad or immersing us in a bubbling cauldron or maelstrom rather than referring to a chronological scheme.

In a very interesting paper in the *International Journal of Psycho-Analysis* in 1990, Ruth Stein took 'A New Look at the Theory of Melanie Klein'.[69] She argues that Klein's is fundamentally a theory of affect in which the focus is 'shifted from Freud's cathectic explanations to the concepts of objects and the feelings attached to them'.[70] 'Positions' become more important than structures, and these are 'built around different core feelings'.[71] There are basically two psychological configurations, corresponding to the two basic instincts. They 'differ fundamentally according to *the capacity of* the individual to tolerate unpleasant or conflictual feelings'.[72] Psychic life is the regulation of feelings.[73] She concludes that 'Klein has no theory of the mental apparatus, and feelings are not placed in any such frame'.[74] Anxiety and guilt are the inevitable outcome of the coexistence of love and hate, and the Oedipal situation generates them.[75]

What I find helpful about this point of view on Klein is that it – along with my own distinction between background and foreground – helps me to understand why I cannot find my way around using a map of the Freudian structures with which I was educated in my original reading of psychoanalysis in an American neo-Freudian context. Kleinian explanations ring true for me. They did when I was an analysand and continue to do so for me as a therapist and supervisor in individual therapy, group therapy and group relations work. In fact, group relations work was founded on the very point I am making here. Klein's distinguished analysand and perhaps the most original thinker in her lineage, Wilfred R. Bion, said in *Experiences in Groups* that there is nothing wrong with Freud's explanations in terms of id, ego and superego (which Freud insisted explained all individual and social phenomena) except that they didn't go deep enough and thereby missed out the 'ultimate sources' of group behaviour, just as they did the behaviour of individuals.[76] What he pointed to as more basic were psychotic anxieties, along with the paranoid-schizoid and depressive positions – and the emotions and basic assumptions that are derived from them and sunder sensible work in groups from time to time.[77]

I have so far tried to do two things concerning Kleinian ideas about the Oedipal dynamic. First, I have sketched Kleinian views on the Oedipus complex and how they differ from Freudian ones. Second, I have offered a couple of ideas which may help us to understand why these two ways of thinking about human nature seem so hard to bring into one framework of ideas – why they are so hard to mesh. I think it is because the fundamental determinants of human nature which are emphasised in the respective frameworks are on different levels. For Klein what matters is always the primitive processes, and the task is never-ending. What matters for Freudians, as Freud put it, is that, 'Where id is, there ego shall be. It's reclamation work, like draining the Zuider Zee.'[78] Some Freudians believe that you can resolve the Oedipus complex. Kleinians believe that you will be faced again and again with the Oedipal situation, more like Sisyphus than Prometheus.

Challenges to Developmental Determinism

The Kleinian position in the matter of developmental determinism is difficult, perhaps impossible, to square with recent arguments on behalf of 'plastic sexuality', whereby gays, lesbians and bisexuals claim that one can refuse the Oedipal path and choose another developmental trajectory.[79] The Kleinian view, according to some, makes the Oedipal configuration something one cannot evade and be a thoughtful, creative person. Of course, it is appropriate to show how failure to work through the Oedipal situation can, indeed, lead to perverse sexuality, as David Morgan has illustrated with moving case material.[80] However, there is in some Kleinian writing the tacit assumption that gay and lesbian sexuality is inherently ill, a position Freud never held. He regarded 'any established aberration from normal sexuality as an instance of developmental inhibition and infantilism'.[81] On the other hand, he did not regard homosexuality or perversion as illnesses.[82]

I am glad to say that some other Kleinians take a different view from the Kleinian orthodoxy and direct our attention to the qualities of unconscious phantasies rather than to sexual behaviours. In some

'Reflections on Perverse States of Mind', Margot Waddell and Gianna Williams argue that perversion of character involves 'the distortion and misuse of psychic and external reality: the slaughter of truth'.[83] Perverse states of mind involve 'a negativistic caricature of object relations'. There is an unconscious 'core phantasy of the secret killing of babies instead of parenting babies – an oblique form of attack on the inside of the mother's body . . . In this frame of reference, perversity has no connection with descriptive aspects of sexual choices – it can be equally present or absent in heterosexual or homosexual relationships alike'.[84] They conclude that this approach is:

. . . *scintillating with possibilities for better understanding the nature of perversity as an aspect of character, as distinct from sexual behaviour or choice. It wholly subverts the current propensity to attach labels of 'perverse' or 'non-perverse' to categories of relationships – e.g., homosexual or heterosexual – and places the distinctions, rather, in the area of psychic reality and meanings as represented by different states of mind.*[85]

So, even when faced with behaviour which appears on the surface to some observers to be *inherently* perverse, one is still left with the clinical task of coming to understand the inner meaning, the object relations and unconscious phantasies, before diagnosing it as pathological. Perverse states of mind are one thing, while 'perversion' is a term that should be used with great care.

Anti-Naturalistic Critiques of the Oedipus Complex

Object Relations Theory

Where Kleinians have made the Oedipus complex much broader and have put the classical chronology of the libido theory in the background, advocates of various other persuasions have gone on to attack the concept and the assumptions underlying it. Certain broad – and other particular – developments in psychoanalysis can be seen as compatible with a very different approach to sexuality than that held by the heirs to Freudian orthodoxy. The broad movement is the decline in adherence to biologism and classical libido theory, and the rise of object relations. Object relations theory developed in the work of Melanie

Klein, Ronald Fairbairn and Donald Winnicott.[86] There are important differences between their formulations (for example, Fairbairn was explicitly turning his back on biology in a way which Klein did not), but the effect on psychoanalytic thinking was to point to relations with the good and bad aspects of the mother and other important figures and part-objects, and to treat relations with objects, rather than the expression of instincts, as the basic preoccupation of psychoanalytic thinking and clinical work. The focus is on relations rather than drives, on *'the object* of my affection [who] can change my complexion from white to rosy red' (as the song says), *rather than the aim* of the instinct as specified in a biologistic metapsychology.[87] Once you do this, sex, sexuality, sexual body parts and sexual energy no longer provide either the rhetoric or the conceptual framework for how we think about the inner world. Love, hatred, unconscious phantasy, anxiety and defences have come to the foreground.[88] For Freud, 'sexual' was all-embracing and meant any attribute of living tissue expressing negative entropy. This is what he meant by 'libido'.[89] Object relations theorists approach the matter the other way round: libido is not seen as pleasure-seeking but object-seeking.[90] Libido does not determine object relations; object relations determine libido.[91] It has been my recent experience that sex in its narrow sense plays a surprisingly small role in psychotherapy training and supervision and the literature. Indeed, some years ago I went to a public lecture by a psychoanalyst, Dr Dennis Duncan, with the title, 'What Ever Happened to Sex in Psychoanalysis?' Along with the turn away from the libido theory has come less attention to the psychosexual developmental scheme and the fairly strict chronology which it specified. As I said, if you read Klein and her followers, you find phrases like 'oral, anal and phallic elements' jumbled up and part of a *potpourri*. What emerged later in their scheme at specified developmental and chronological points in the libido theory somehow gets mixed in at an earlier stage in Klein's approach.

Alternative Developmental Schemes

The turn away from the libido theory and towards object relations theory is relevant to the topic of alternative developmental paths. Some of the most interesting writers in this debate make this their most important point: 'What's so wonderful about the developmental path specified by the libido theory?' In asking this question, they are attacking the centrality of the Oedipus complex in orthodox Freudianism. They write in explicit opposition to the Freudian 'Law of the Father' on which the importance of the Oedipus complex is based.[92] As the gay theorist John Fletcher puts it:

What is refused here is not masculinity or the phallus in itself, but the polarity at the heart of the Oedipal injunction: 'You cannot be what you desire, you cannot desire what you wish to be.'[93]

What the Freudians claim as natural is what the sexual dissidents attack as a cultural norm to be struggled against. They argue for a re-symbolisation and re-investment in a new kind of sexuality. However, Freud himself said that:

... a disposition to perversions is an original and universal disposition of the human sexual instinct and that normal sexual behaviour is developed out of it as a result of organic changes and psychical inhibitions during the course of development ... Among the forces restricting the direction taken by the sexual instinct we laid emphasis upon shame, disgust, pity and

the structures of morality and authority erected by society.[94]

Support for this approach is found in the writings of the eminent French psychoanalyst, Jean Laplanche. The list of erogenous zones specified by the libido theory – mouth, anus, urethra, genitals – is accepted, but they are described less biologistically as places of exchange between inside and outside.[95] However, *any* bodily zone can take on a sexual level of excitement, as can ideas. The traditional understanding of perversion is an alteration or deviation from the fixed, biologically determined order of privileged zones, culminating in genital intercourse to orgasm. But if we refuse to accept this spontaneous unfolding of a unitary instinctual programme, sexuality itself can be seen as polymorphous and therefore, to put it ironically, perverse. Laplanche expresses this starkly by saying that:

[T]*he* exception – *i.e., the perversion – ends up by* taking the rule along with it. *The exception, which should presuppose the existence of a definite instinct, a pre-existent sexual function, with its well-defined norms of accomplishment: that exception ends up by undermining and destroying the very notion of a biological norm. The whole of sexuality, or at least the whole of infantile sexuality, ends up becoming perversion.*[96]

Fletcher puts this in symbolic terms, terms which increase the range, scope and flexibility of sexuality: 'The whole of sexuality as a mobile field of displace-able and substitutable signs and mental representa-tions is a *perversion* of the order of biological needs and fixed objects.'[97] If perversion is ubiquitous, it cannot be called exceptional; it is commonplace, the rule, normal – hence 'perversion' as 'normal'. The pejorative connotations of the term become obsolete and, marching to the strict developmental require-ments of the libido theory – with the Oedipus complex at its heart, it loses its authoritarian legiti-macy and theoretical underpinnings.

Writing about bisexuality and lesbianism, Beverly Burch takes a similar line in opposition to biologism and in favour of social constructivism. She says that: 'Lesbianism *and* heterosexual identities are social constructs that incorporate psychological elements.'[98] These differ from one woman to another and have manifestations and sources as varied as individual biographies: 'The unity of heterosexual theory does not live up to the diversity of sexual orientations.'[99] She places sexual orientations on a continuum and argues that any point on it might be defensive, 'no position is necessarily or inevitably pathological'.[100] She surveys the literature and finds a relativism of theory to match her relativism of developmental pathways:

The point is that no one view is complete, and there are divergent routes on the way to final object choice. The road is not a straight one towards heterosexuality, and we cannot regard other destinations as a wrong turn.[101]

Writers on these issues draw different lines between what they consider pathological and what they treat as merely human diversity. Robert Stoller defines perversion as 'the erotic form of hatred' and offers critical analyses of fetishism, rape, sexually motivated murder, sadism, masochism, voyeurism and paedophilia. He sees in each of these 'hostility, revenge, triumph and a dehumanised object'.[102] On the subject of homosexuality, however, he is a champion of pluralism:

What evidence is there that heterosexuality is less complicated than homosexuality, less a product of infantile-childhood struggles to master trauma, conflict, frustration, and the like? As a result of innumerable analyses, the burden of proof . . . has shifted to those who use the heterosexual as the standard of health, normality, mature genital characterhood, or whatever other ambiguous criterion serves one's philosophy these days . . . Thus far, the counting, if it is done from published reports, puts the heterosexual and the homosexual in a tie: 100 percent abnormals.[103]

Another gem from Stoller is:

Beware the concept 'normal,' it is beyond the reach of objectivity. It tries to connote statistical validity but hides brute judgements on social and private goodness that, if admitted, would promote honesty and modesty we do not yet have in patriots, lawmakers, psychoanalysts and philosophers.[104]

Once again, with the rise in pluralism about alternative developmental schemes goes, for some, a demise in belief in the developmental pathway of the orthodox libido theory within which the Oedipus complex is the most important maturational rite of passage. Most psychoanalytically oriented practitioners would not be willing to go all the way down this path towards social constructivism in their approaches to development. An American neo-Freudian compendium, published in 1990, which purports to provide an integration of recent views, reports without comment: 'Indeed, [Leo] Rangell described the Oedipus complex as the climax of infantile instinctual life, the nucleus of the neuroses and the "organizing umbrella of future life".'[105]

Conclusion

I have tried to provide an exposition of the original idea of the Oedipus complex. Even though Freud claimed it as the basic concept in psychoanalysis, he never drew his thinking on the concept to a final formulation. There are many loose ends. Second, I have presented some ideas of Klein and later Kleinians in which the developmental scheme of the libido theory is placed in the background while Oedipal dynamics are broadened out into an 'Oedipal situation' which recurs throughout life. This less biologistic and more object-related idea is also linked to maturation of insight and to the paranoid-schizoid and depressive positions. Finally, I have sketched ideas about gender development whose proponents reject any notion of privileged developmental paths. Indeed, increasingly sophisticated theorisations of gay and lesbian views on gender identity have reached the point where they can claim that the exceptions overwhelm the rule, and can put forward the long-term goal of 'eschewing all forms of naturalism in psychoanalytic thinking'.[106] Exit the Oedipus complex.

My own view of the matter does not go that far. I find the original notion of the Oedipus complex inside the strict chronology of the libido theory too concrete and restrictive, too linked to specific body parts; although I should add that I often think of where a patient is developmentally and what stages he or she may have passed or be stuck at. More importantly, I have increasingly found that thinking in terms of the Oedipal situation – and difficulties in working through it – is appropriate in all my clinical work. In my opinion, the Oedipus complex belongs with the idea of the Unconscious and the concept of projective identification as one of the three most fruitful ideas in psychoanalysis. I have reached the conclusion that coming to understand the specific Oedipal dynamic between each of my patients and his or her parents (step-parents, children, etc.) lies at the centre of unravelling the tangles which have caused them anguish and have restricted their access to a fuller use of their capacities.

A Closing Note on Sophocles

When I read of Jocasta's last agony, an old joke I'd recalled about Oedipus was suddenly not so funny: 'There she bewailed the twice confounded issue of her wifehood – husband begotten of husband, child of child.'[107] And 'worse was yet to see'[108] when Oedipus found her, cut her body down and blinded himself with her golden brooches. I remembered that we are here in the realm of actual and phantasied violence, child abuse and incest, sometimes nominally consenting, usually coerced, leaving deep scars. The failures to negotiate this complex are myriad in the present and throughout history. I think Kleinian psycho-analysis has shown that it is a never-ending battle, as we move back and forth – sometimes moment by moment and surely at every challenge-point in life – between fragmentation and integration, blaming and reparation, hate and love.

We can make a choice of levels. The first is the Yiddisha momma who brings her son to the psychologist, who examines the boy and calls the mother in to announce gravely that he has an Oedipus complex, to which she replies: 'Oedipus, Schmeedipus, as long as he loves his mother.' The historic Mrs Oedipus, the queen Jocasta, was equally keen to avoid deeper truths:

Fear? What has a man to do with fear?
Chance rules our lives, and the future is all unknown.
Best live as best we may, from day to day.
Nor need this mother-marrying frighten you;
Many a man has dreamt as much. Such things
Must be forgotten, if life is to be endured.[109]

Sophocles offers another punchline, one which evokes the tragedy in every life, where, as Teiresias put it,[110] each is the enemy of himself, as well as detective and criminal:

Sons and daughters of Thebes, behold: this was
    Oedipus,
Greatest of men; he held the key to the deepest
    mysteries;

*Was envied by all his fellow-men for his great
  prosperity;*
*Behold, what a full tide of misfortune swept over his
  head.*
*Then learn that mortal man must always look to his
  ending,*
*And none can be called happy until that day when he
  carries*
His happiness down to the grave in peace.[111]

Further Reading

For all references, place of publication is London unless otherwise indicated.

Abel-Hirsch, Nicola, *Eros*, Cambridge: Icon Books, 2001.

Abelove, Henry, 'Freud, Homosexuality and the Americans', *Dissent*, Winter 1986, pp. 59–69.

Abraham, Karl, 'Psycho-Analytical Studies on Character-Formation' (1921–5), in *Selected Papers on Psycho-Analysis,* Maresfield, 1979, pp. 370–418.

—— 'A Short Study of the Development of the Libido, Viewed in the Light of Mental Disorders' (1924), in *Selected Papers on Psycho-Analysis,* Maresfield, 1979, pp. 418–501.

—— *Selected Papers on Psycho-Analysis*, Maresfield, 1979.

Anzieu, Didier, *Freud's Self-Analysis,* Hogarth, 1986 (esp. Chapter 3).

Bell, David, 'Hysteria – A Contemporary Kleinian Perspective', *British Journal of Psychotherapy*, vol. 9, 1992, pp. 169–80.

Bergmann, Martin S., *The Anatomy of Loving: The Story of Man's Quest to Know What Love Is*, Columbia, 1987.

Bion, Wilfred R., 'Group Dynamics – A Re-view', in Klein, Melanie, et al. (eds.), *New Directions in Psycho-Analysis: The Significance of Infant Conflict in the Patterns of Adult Behaviour*, Tavistock, 1955, pp. 440–77; reprinted by Maresfield, 1977.

—— *Experiences in Groups and Other Papers*, Tavistock, 1961.

Brenner, Charles, *An Elementary Textbook of Psycho-analysis*, revised edition, New York: International Universities, 1973.

Britton, Ronald, 'The Missing Link: Parental Sexuality in the Oedipus Complex', in Britton et al., *The Oedipus Complex Today: Clinical Implications*, Karnac, 1989, pp. 83–102.

—— 'The Oedipus Situation and the Depressive Position', in Anderson, Robin (ed.), *Clinical Lectures on Klein and Bion*, intro. by Hanna Segal, Routledge, 1992, pp. 34–45.

—— et al., *The Oedipus Complex Today: Clinical Implications*, Karnac, 1989.

Burch, Beverly, 'Heterosexuality, Bisexuality, and Lesbianism: Psychoanalytic Views of Women's Sexual Object Choice', *Psychoanalytic Review*, vol. 80, 1993, pp. 83–100.

—— *On Intimate Terms: The Psychology of Difference in Lesbian Relationships*, Illinois, 1993a.

Chasseguet-Smirgel, Janine, *Creativity and Perversion*, Free Association Books, 1985.

—— *The Ego Ideal: A Psychoanalytic Essay on the Malady of the Ideal*, Free Association Books, 1985a.

Chodorow, Nancy, *The Reproduction of Mothering: Psychoanalysis and the Sociology of Gender*, University of California, 1978.

Cornwell, Joan, 'The Establishment of Female Genital Sexuality', *Free Associations*, no. 1, 1985, pp. 57–75.

Dinnerstein, Dorothy, *The Mermaid and the Minotaur:*

Sexual Arrangements and Human Malaise, New York: Harper and Row, 1976.

Erikson, Erik H., *Identity and the Life Cycle: Selected Papers,* in *Psychological Issues,* vol. 1, no. 1, monograph 1, International Universities, 1959. Reissued as *Identity and the Life Cycle*, New York: W.W. Norton, 1994.

Fletcher, John, 'Freud and His Uses: Psychoanalysis and Gay Theory', in Simon Shepherd and Mick Wallis (eds.), *Coming on Strong: Gay Politics and Culture*, Unwin Hyman, 1989, pp. 90–118.

Fletchman Smith, Barbara, *Mental Slavery: Psychoanalytic Studies of Caribbean People*, Rebus, 2000.

Freud, Sigmund, *The Standard Edition of the Complete Psychological Works of Sigmund Freud*, 24 vols., Hogarth, 1953–73. (Hereafter, *SE*.)

—— *The Interpretation of Dreams* (1900), *SE*, vols. 4 and 5.

—— *Three Essays on the Theory of Sexuality* (1905), *SE*, vol. 7, pp. 125–245.

—— 'A Special Type of Choice of Object Made by Men' (1910), *SE*, vol. 11, pp. 163–76.

—— *Totem and Taboo* (1913), *SE*, vol. 13, pp. 1–162.

—— 'Observations on Transference Love: Further Recommendations on the Technique of Psycho-Analysis III' (1915), *SE*, vol. 12, pp. 159–71.

—— 'Preface to Reik's *Ritual: Psycho-Analytic Studies*' (1919), *SE*, vol. 17, pp. 256–63.

—— *The Ego and the Id* (1923), *SE*, vol. 19, pp. 3–66.

—— 'The Infantile Genital Organization: An Interpolation into the Theory of Sexuality' (1923a), *SE*, vol. 19, pp. 141–8.

—— 'The Dissolution of the Oedipus Complex' (1924), *SE*, vol. 19, pp. 171–9.

—— 'Some Psychical Consequences of the Anatomical Distinction Between the Sexes' (1925), *SE*, vol. 19, pp. 243–60.

—— *Civilization and Its Discontents* (1930), *SE*, vol. 21, pp. 59–145.

—— 'Female Sexuality' (1931), *SE*, vol. 21, pp. 223–43.

—— *New Introductory Lectures on Psycho-Analysis* (1933), *SE*, vol. 22, pp. 3–182.

—— *Extracts from the Fliess Papers* (1950), *SE*, vol. 1, pp. 175–280.

Giddens, Anthony, *The Transformation of Intimacy: Sexuality, Love and Eroticism in Modern Societies*, Polity, 1992; paperback edition, 1993.

Green, André, 'The Dead Mother', in *On Private Madness*, Hogarth, 1986, pp. 142–73.

Greenberg, Jay R., *Oedipus and Beyond: A Clinical Theory*, Harvard, 1991.

—— and Mitchell, Stephen A., *Object Relations in Psycho-analytic Theory*, Harvard, 1983.

Hamilton, Victoria, *Narcissus and Oedipus: The Children of Psychoanalysis,* Routledge, 1982; reprinted by Karnac, 1993.

Hinshelwood, R.D., 'Oedipus Complex', in *A Dictionary*

of Kleinian Thought, revised edition, Free Association Books, 1991, pp. 57–67.

Johnson, Allen W., and Price-Williams, Douglass, *Oedipus Ubiquitous: The Family Complex in World Folk Literature*, Stanford: Stanford University Press, 1996.

Jones, Ernest, *Hamlet and Oedipus*, New York: Doubleday Anchor, 1949.

King, Pearl, and Steiner, Ricardo (eds.), *The Freud–Klein Controversies: 1941–45*, Tavistock/Routledge, 1991.

Klein, Melanie, 'Early Stages of the Oedipus Conflict', *International Journal of Psycho-Analysis*, vol. 9, 1928, 167–80; reprinted in *The Writings of Melanie Klein*, Hogarth, vol. 1, 1975, pp. 186–98.

—— 'The Oedipus Complex in the Light of Early Anxieties', *International Journal of Psycho-Analysis*, vol. 26, 1945, pp. 11–33; reprinted in Klein (1975), vol. 1, pp. 370–419, and in Britton et al. (1989), pp. 11–82 (see esp. summary, pp. 63–82).

—— 'Notes on Some Schizoid Mechanisms', *International Journal of Psycho-Analysis*, vol. 27, 1946, pp. 99–110; reprinted in Klein (1975), vol. 3, pp. 1–24.

—— *The Writings of Melanie Klein*, 5 vols., Hogarth, 1975.

—— et al. (eds.), *New Directions in Psycho-Analysis: The Significance of Infant Conflict in the Patterns of Adult Behaviour*, Tavistock, 1977; reprinted by Maresfield, 1977.

Laplanche, Jean, *Life and Death in Psychoanalysis* (1970), Johns Hopkins University Press, 1976; paperback edition, 1985.

—— and Pontalis, J.-B., *The Language of Psychoanalysis*, Hogarth, 1973.

Limentani, Adam, 'The Oedipus Myth as Reflected in Problems of Ambivalence and Reparation in the Oedipal Situation', in *Between Freud and Klein: The Psychoanalytic Quest for Knowledge and Truth*, Free Association Books, 1989, pp. 18–34.

Meltzer, Donald, *Sexual States of Mind*, Strath Tay: Clunie, 1973.

Mitchell, Juliet, *Psychoanalysis and Feminism*, Allen Lane, 1974.

—— *Mad Men and Medusas: Reclaiming Hysteria and the Effects of Sibling Relationships on the Human Condition*, Allen Lane/The Penguin Press, 2000.

Morgan, David, 'The Internal Couple and the Oedipus Complex in the Development of Sexual Identity and Sexual Perversion', in Harding, Celia (ed.), *Sexuality: Psychoanalytic Perspectives*, Brunner-Routledge, 2001, pp. 137–52.

Mullahy, Patrick, *Oedipus – Myth and Complex: A Review of Psychoanalytic Theory*, New York: Grove Press, 1948; reprinted, 1955.

Nagera, Humberto (ed.), *Basic Psychoanalytic Concepts on the Libido Theory*, Unwin Hyman, 1969; reprinted by Karnac as paperback edition, 1981, 1990.

O'Connor, Noreen, and Ryan, Joanna, *Wild Desires and Mistaken Identities: Lesbianism and Psychoanalysis*, Virago, 1993.

Pollock, George H., and Ross, John M., *The Oedipus Papers*, Madison: International Universities Press, 1988.

Rangell, Leo, 'Aggression, Oedipus and Historical Perspective', *International Journal of Psycho-Analysis*, vol. 53, 1972, pp. 3–11.

Rapaport, David, *The Collected Papers of David Rapaport*, New York: Basic, 1967.

—— and Gill, Merton M., 'The Points of View and Assumptions of Metapsychology', *International Journal of Psycho-Analysis*, vol. 40, 1959, pp. 1–10.

Roland, Alan, *In Search of Self in India and Japan*, Princeton, 1988.

Rudnytsky, Peter L., *Freud and Oedipus*, New York: Columbia, 1987.

—— and Spitz, Ellen H. (eds.), *Freud and Forbidden Knowledge*, New York University Press, 1994.

Simon, Bennett, 'Is the Oedipus Complex Still the Cornerstone of Psychoanalysis?: Three Obstacles to Answering the Question', *Journal of the American Psychoanalytic Association*, vol. 39, 1991, pp. 641–68.

Sophocles, *The Theban Plays*, trans. E.F. Watling, Penguin, 1947.

Stein, Ruth, 'A New Look at the Theory of Melanie Klein', *International Journal of Psycho-Analysis*, vol. 71, 1990, pp. 499–511.

Steiner, John, 'Turning a Blind Eye: The Cover Up for Oedipus', *International Review of Psycho-Analysis*, vol. 12, 1985, pp. 161–72.

Stoller, Robert J., *Observing the Erotic Imagination*, Yale, 1985.

—— *Perversion: The Erotic Form of Hatred*, Maresfield, 1975; paperback edition, 1986.

Temperley, Jane, 'Is the Oedipus Complex Bad News for Women?', *Free Associations*, vol. 30, 1993, pp. 265–75.

Tyson, Phyllis, and Tyson, Robert L., *Psychoanalytic Theories of Development: An Integration*, Yale, 1990.

Waddell, Margot, 'Gender Identity: Fifty Years On From Freud', *British Journal of Psychotherapy*, vol. 5, 1989, pp. 381–9; reprinted in *Women: A Cultural Review,* vol. 1, 1990, pp. 149–59.

—— 'From Resemblance to Identity: A Psychoanalytic Perspective on Gender Identity', typescript, 1992.

—— and Williams, Gianna, 'Reflections on Perverse States of Mind', *Free Associations*, vol. 2, 1991, pp. 203–13.

Young, Robert M., 'Consider Laius', *Free Associations*, no. 13, 1988, p. 150.

—— *Mental Space*, Process Press, 1994.

—— 'Is "Perversion" Obsolete?', *Psychology in Society*, vol. 21, 1996, pp. 5–26.

Notes

For all references, place of publication is London unless otherwise indicated.

1. See Chasseguet-Smirgel, Janine, *Creativity and Perversion*, Free Association Books, 1985; *The Ego Ideal: A Psychoanalytic Essay on the Malady of the Ideal*, Free Association Books, 1985a.

2. Bergmann, Martin S., *The Anatomy of Loving: The Story of Man's Quest to Know What Love Is*, Columbia, 1987, Chapter 18.

3. Ibid., p. 220.

4. Ibid., p. 222.

5. Ibid., p. 223.

6. Freud, Sigmund, 'Observations on Transference Love: Further Recommendations on the Technique of Psycho-Analysis III' (1915), in *The Standard Edition of the Complete Psychological Works of Sigmund Freud*, Hogarth, 1953–73 (hereafter, *SE*), vol. 12, pp. 159–71 (p. 166).

7. See Brenner, Charles, *An Elementary Textbook of Psychoanalysis*, revised edition, New York: International Universities, 1973, p. 26; and Meltzer, Donald, *Sexual States of Mind*, Strath Tay: Clunie, 1973, pp. 21–7.

8. Cf. Dinnerstein, Dorothy, *The Mermaid and the Minotaur: Sexual Arrangements and Human Malaise*, New York: Harper and Row, 1976; and Chodorow, Nancy, *The Reproduction of Mothering: Psychoanalysis and the*

Sociology of Gender, University of California, 1978.

9. Cornwell, Joan, 'The Establishment of Female Genital Sexuality', *Free Associations*, vol. 1, 1985, pp. 57–75; Waddell, Margot, 'From Resemblance to Identity: A Psychoanalytic Perspective on Gender Identity', typescript, 1992, esp. pp. 9–10.

10. Erikson, Erik H., *Identity and the Life Cycle: Selected Papers*, in *Psychological Issues,* vol. 1, no. 1, monograph 1, International Universities, 1959, p. 120. Reissued as *Identity and the Life Cycle*, New York: W.W. Norton, 1994.

11. Nagera, Humberto (ed.), *Basic Psychoanalytic Concepts on the Libido Theory*, Unwin Hyman, 1969, pp. 64–82.

12. Laplanche, Jean, and Pontalis, J.-B., *The Language of Psychoanalysis*, Hogarth, 1973, pp. 282–7.

13. See also Mullahy, Patrick, *Oedipus – Myth and Complex: A Review of Psychoanalytic Theory*, New York: Grove Press, 1955, pp. 20–7.

14. Freud, Sigmund, *New Introductory Lectures on Psycho-Analysis* (1933), *SE*, vol. 22, pp. 3–182 (p. 113).

15. See Klein, Melanie, 'The Oedipus Complex in the Light of Early Anxieties' (1945), in Britton, Ronald, et al., *The Oedipus Complex Today: Clinical Implications*, Karnac, 1989, pp. 11–82 (pp. 72–5); Mitchell, Juliet, *Psychoanalysis and Feminism*, Allen Lane, 1974; Dinnerstein (1976); Temperley, Jane, 'Is the Oedipus Complex Bad News for Women?', *Free Associations*, vol.

30, part 4, 1993, pp. 265–75.

16. Fletchman Smith, Barbara, *Mental Slavery: Psycho-analytic Studies of Caribbean People*, Rebus, 2000.

17. Those interested in pursuing the fine texture of the debates about formulations of the Oedipus complex should consult, *inter alia,* Sigmund Freud ('The Infantile Genital Organization: An Interpolation into the Theory of Sexuality' (1923), *SE*, vol. 19, pp. 141–8; 'The Dissolution of the Oedipus Complex' (1924), *SE*, vol. 19, pp. 171–9; 'Some Psychical Consequences of the Anatomical Distinction Between the Sexes' (1925), *SE*, vol. 19, pp. 243–60); Karl Abraham ('Psycho-Analytical Studies on Character-Formation' (1921–5), in *Selected Papers on Psycho-Analysis,* Maresfield, 1979, pp. 370–418; 'A Short Study of the Development of the Libido, Viewed in the Light of Mental Disorders' (1924), in Abraham (1979), pp. 418–501); Victoria Hamilton (*Narcissus and Oedipus: The Children of Psychoanalysis*, Routledge, 1982); Adam Limentani ('The Oedipus Myth as Reflected in Problems of Ambivalence and Reparation in the Oedipal Situation', in *Between Freud and Klein: The Psychoanalytic Quest for Knowledge and Truth*, Free Association Books, 1989, pp. 18–34); George H. Pollock and John M. Ross (*The Oedipus Papers*, Madison: International Universities Press, 1988); Bennett Simon ('Is the Oedipus Complex Still the Cornerstone of Psychoanalysis?: Three Obstacles to Answering the Question', *Journal of the American Psychoanalytic Association*, vol. 39, 1991, pp. 641–68); Jay R.

Greenberg (*Oedipus and Beyond: A Clinical Theory*, Harvard, 1991); and Juliet Mitchell (*Mad Men and Medusas: Reclaiming Hysteria and the Effects of Sibling Relationships on the Human Condition*, Allen Lane: The Penguin Press, 2000).

18. Freud, Sigmund, *Three Essays on the Theory of Sexuality* (1905), *SE*, vol. 7, pp. 125–245 (p. 226n).

19. Ibid., pp. 225, 225n.

20. Freud, Sigmund, *Civilization and Its Discontents* (1930), *SE*, vol. 21, pp. 59–145 (p. 60).

21. Ibid., p. 131.

22. Ibid., p. 134.

23. See, e.g., Mullahy (1955), pp. 323–4; Johnson, Allen W., and Price-Williams, Douglass, *Oedipus Ubiquitous: The Family Complex in World Folk Literature*, Stanford: Stanford University Press, 1996, pp. 14ff.

24. Johnson and Price-Williams (1996), p. 6.

25. Freud, Sigmund, 'Preface to Reik's *Ritual: Psycho-Analytic Studies*' (1919), *SE*, vol. 17, pp. 256–63 (pp. 261–2).

26. Ibid.

27. Freud, Sigmund, *The Interpretation of Dreams* (1900), *SE*, vols. 4 and 5, pp. 263–4.

28. Freud, Sigmund, *The Ego and the Id* (1923), *SE*, vol. 19, pp. 3–66.

29. For further information on Klein's concept of the position, see Abel-Hirsch, Nicola, *Eros*, Cambridge: Icon Books, 2001, pp. 38–9.

30. See Freud (1900), pp. 264–6; Jones, Ernest, *Hamlet and Oedipus*, New York: Doubleday Anchor, 1949.

31. Sophocles, *King Oedipus,* in *The Theban Plays*, trans. E.F. Watling, Penguin, 1947, p. 45.

32. Ibid., p. 47.

33. Ibid., p. 47.

34. Ibid., p. 48.

35. Young, Robert M., 'Consider Laius', *Free Associations*, vol. 13, 1988, p. 150.

36. Steiner, John, 'Turning a Blind Eye: The Cover Up for Oedipus', *International Review of Psycho-Analysis*, vol. 12, 1985, pp. 161–72.

37. See Klein, Melanie: 'Early Stages of the Oedipus Conflict' (1928), in *The Writings of Melanie Klein*, Hogarth, vol. 1, 1975, pp. 186–98; 'The Oedipus Complex in the Light of Early Anxieties' (1945), in Klein (1975), vol. 1, pp. 370–419; 'Notes on Some Schizoid Mechanisms' (1946), in Klein (1975), vol. 3, pp. 1–24.

38. Freud, Sigmund, *Extracts from the Fliess Papers* (1950), *SE*, vol. 1, pp. 175–280 (p. 265).

39. Cf. Freud (1900), pp. 263–6.

40. Freud (1900), pp. 262–3.

41. Ibid., p. 263n.

42. Freud (1910); Freud (1913).

43. Rudnytsky, Peter L., *Freud and Oedipus*, New York: Columbia, 1987, p. 15.

44. Ibid., pp. 11–12. See also Rudnytsky, Peter L., and

Spitz, Ellen H. (eds.), *Freud and Forbidden Knowledge*, New York University Press, 1994.

45. Rudnytsky (1987), pp. 4–5; Anzieu, Didier, *Freud's Self-Analysis,* Hogarth, 1986, Chapter 3.

46. E.g., King, Pearl, and Steiner, Ricardo (eds.), *The Freud–Klein Controversies: 1941–45*, Tavistock/Routledge, 1991, pp. 432–3.

47. Such a rendition can be found in two places – at the end of Klein's 1945 paper, 'The Oedipus Complex in the Light of Early Anxieties' (reprinted in Britton et al.'s collection, *The Oedipus Complex Today* (1989), summary, pp. 63–82). An up-to-date exposition is available in the entry on 'Oedipus Complex' in R.D. Hinshelwood's *A Dictionary of Kleinian Thought*, (revised edition, Free Association Books, 1991, pp. 57–67), and the issues are broadened and deepened in two papers by Ronald Britton ('The Missing Link: Parental Sexuality in the Oedipus Complex', in Britton et al. (1989), pp. 83–102; 'The Oedipus Situation and the Depressive Position', in Anderson, Robin (ed.), *Clinical Lectures on Klein and Bion*, Routledge, 1992, pp. 34–45) and one by David Bell ('Hysteria – A Contemporary Kleinian Perspective', *British Journal of Psychotherapy*, vol. 9, 1992, pp. 169–80).

48. Klein (1945), in Britton et al. (1989), p. 76.

49. Ibid., pp. 76–7.

50. Ibid., p. 78.

51. Ibid., p. 78.

52. Ibid., p. 79.

53. Ibid., p. 82.

54. Ibid., pp. 81–2.

55. Klein (1946), p. 8.

56. Bell, David, 'Hysteria – A Contemporary Kleinian Perspective', *British Journal of Psychotherapy*, vol. 9, 1992, pp. 169–80 (p. 172).

57. Ibid.

58. Britton, Ronald, 'The Oedipus Situation and the Depressive Position', in Anderson, Robin (ed.), *Clinical Lectures on Klein and Bion*, Routledge, 1992, pp. 34–45 (p. 35).

59. Ibid., p. 37.

60. Ibid., p. 39.

61. Ibid., p. 38.

62. Britton, Ronald, 'The Missing Link: Parental Sexuality in the Oedipus Complex', in Britton et al. (1989), pp. 83–102 (p. 87).

63. King and Steiner (1991).

64. Hinshelwood, R.D., 'Oedipus Complex', in Hinshelwood (1991), p. 57.

65. Ibid., p. 60.

66. Green, André, 'The Dead Mother', in *On Private Madness*, Hogarth, 1986, pp. 142–73.

67. Chasseguet-Smirgel (1985a).

68. See Rapaport, David, and Gill, Merton M., 'The Points of View and Assumptions of Metapsychology', *International Journal of Psycho-Analysis*, vol. 40, 1959,

pp. 1–10; Rapaport, David, *The Collected Papers of David Rapaport*, New York: Basic, 1967.

69. Stein, Ruth, 'A New Look at the Theory of Melanie Klein', *International Journal of Psycho-Analysis*, vol. 71, 1990, pp. 499–511.

70. Ibid., p. 500.

71. Ibid., p. 504.

72. Ibid., pp. 504–5 (emphasis in original).

73. Ibid., p. 508.

74. Ibid., p. 509.

75. Ibid., p. 505.

76. Bion, Wilfred R.: 'Group Dynamics – A Re-view', in Klein, Melanie, et al. (eds.), *New Directions in Psycho-Analysis: The Significance of Infant Conflict in the Patterns of Adult Behaviour*, Tavistock, 1955, pp. 440–77 (pp. 475–6); *Experiences in Groups and Other Papers*, Tavistock, 1961, pp. 187–90.

77. Young, Robert M., *Mental Space*, Process Press, 1994, Chapters 5–7.

78. Freud (1933), p. 80.

79. Giddens, Anthony, *The Transformation of Intimacy: Sexuality, Love and Eroticism in Modern Societies*, Polity, 1992; and Young, Robert M., 'Is "Perversion" Obsolete?', *Psychology in Society*, vol. 21, 1996, pp. 5–26.

80. Morgan, David, 'The Internal Couple and the Oedipus Complex in the Development of Sexual Identity and Sexual Perversion', in Harding, Celia (ed.), *Sexuality:*

Psychoanalytic Perspectives, Brunner-Routledge, 2001, pp. 137–52.

81. Freud (1905), p. 231.

82. Abelove, Henry, 'Freud, Homosexuality and the Americans', *Dissent*, Winter 1986, pp. 59–69 (pp. 59, 60).

83. Waddell, Margot, and Williams, Gianna, 'Reflections on Perverse States of Mind', *Free Associations*, vol. 2, 1991, pp. 203–13 (p. 203).

84. Ibid., p. 206.

85. Ibid., p. 211.

86. Greenberg, Jay R., and Mitchell, Stephen A., *Object Relations in Psychoanalytic Theory*, Harvard, 1983.

87. Ibid., p. 126.

88. Ibid., p. 137.

89. Stoller, Robert J., *Perversion: The Erotic Form of Hatred*, Maresfield, paperback edition, 1986, p. 12.

90. Greenberg and Mitchell (1983), p. 154.

91. Ibid., p. 157.

92. Fletcher, John, 'Freud and His Uses: Psychoanalysis and Gay Theory', in Simon Shepherd and Mick Wallis (eds.), *Coming on Strong: Gay Politics and Culture*, Unwin Hyman, 1989, pp. 90–118 (p. 113).

93. Ibid., p. 114.

94. Freud (1905), p. 231.

95. Fletcher (1989), p. 96.

96. Laplanche, Jean, *Life and Death in Psychoanalysis* (1970), Johns Hopkins University Press, 1976, p. 23.

97. Fletcher (1989), pp. 98–9.

98. Burch, Beverly, 'Heterosexuality, Bisexuality, and Lesbianism: Psychoanalytic Views of Women's Sexual Object Choice', *Psychoanalytic Review*, vol. 80, 1993, pp. 83–100 (pp. 84–5).

99. Ibid., p. 85.

100. Ibid., p. 91.

101. Ibid., p. 97. See also Burch, Beverly, *On Intimate Terms: The Psychology of Difference in Lesbian Relationships*, Illinois, 1993a.

102. Stoller (1986), p. 9.

103. Stoller, Robert J., *Observing the Erotic Imagination*, Yale, 1985. Quoted in Burch (1993), p. 97.

104. Stoller (1985), p. 41. Quoted in Burch (1993), p. 98.

105. Rangell, Leo, 'Aggression, Oedipus and Historical Perspective', *International Journal of Psycho-Analysis*, vol. 53, 1972, pp. 3–11 (p. 7). Quoted in Tyson, Phyllis, and Tyson, Robert L., *Psychoanalytic Theories of Development: An Integration*, Yale, 1990, p. 59.

106. O'Connor, Noreen, and Ryan, Joanna, *Wild Desires and Mistaken Identities: Lesbianism and Psychoanalysis*, Virago, 1993, p. 246.

107. Sophocles (1947), p. 60.

108. Ibid., p. 61.

109. Ibid., p. 52.

110. Ibid., p. 36.

111. Ibid., p. 68.

Acknowledgements

I should like to acknowledge the particularly assiduous and insightful editorial comments and contributions of Ivan Ward.